Loving Jesus
for children

Chelsea Kong

PRINTED IN 2024-2025, MADE IN TORONTO, CANADA
ISBN: 978-1-998335-26-8
LIBRARY AND ARCHIVES CANADA

JESUS LOVES YOU SO MUCH.
HE LOVES TO BE WITH YOU.

THE BIBLE TELLS US ABOUT HIS LOVE.
HIS LOVE IS BIGGER THAN YOUR
DAD'S AND MOM'S LOVE.

LEARN AND KNOW THE BIBLE.
IT IS YOUR SWORD AGAINST SATAN.
HE WILL FIGHT US.

JESUS LOVES IT WHEN WE PRAY.
WE TALK, LISTEN, AND FOLLOW.

HE IS ALWAYS WATCHING.
NOT EVERYONE CAN SEE HIM.

HE LOVES IT WHEN WE SING,
DANCE, PLAY MUSIC, AND MORE.

WE WALK BY FAITH.
WE WATCH OUT FOR DANGER.

**PRAY FOR OTHERS.
PRAY WITH ALL YOUR HEART, SOUL,
MIND, AND STRENGTH.**

WE ARE JESUS' SHEEP.
HE WILL GIVE US WHAT WE NEED.

JESUS IS HUMBLE AND LOVES PEOPLE.
HE RODE ON A DONKEY.

**HE IS OUR SHEPHERD.
HE TEACHES AND CORRECTS US.**

JESUS CALLS US TO SHARE
THE GOOD NEWS WITH OTHERS.

WORSHIP JESUS EVERY DAY.
PRAISE, GIVE THANKS, AND REJOICE!
IN HEAVEN WE WORSHIP EVERY DAY.

JESUS WON AGAINST THE DEVIL.
WE DON'T NEED TO BE AFRAID.
HE WILL NOT LET US BE HAPPY.

JESUS DIED ON THE CROSS FOR US.
HE GIVES US A NEW LIFE.
HE WANTS US TO CARRY OUR CROSS.

JESUS IS KING, AND GOD HATES SIN.
HE WILL JUDGE ALL EVIL.
LOOK AT JESUS FOR EVERYTHING.

DAD AND MOM MUST OBEY GOD.
HE KEEPS THEM TOGETHER.
THEY MUST LOVE EACH OTHER.

CHILDREN MUST OBEY THEIR PARENTS. GOD WILL BLESS YOU MORE.

JESUS KNOWS WHEN TO COME TO US.
WE MUST LOVE AND TRUST HIM.
GOD GIVES US THE BEST.

HOLY SPIRIT GIVES HIS WORDS.
HE TEACHES AND HELPS US.

WE MAY FEEL THAT JESUS DOESN'T
LOVE US, BUT THAT'S A LIE.
THE LORD WILL MAKE US WAIT.

WE NEED TO BE STRONG.
FORGIVE AND ASK FOR HELP.

GOD MIGHT TELL YOU NOT TO EAT
FOR A FEW DAYS OR SAY WHAT HE
DOESN'T WANT YOU TO EAT.

HE SAYS THIS SO THAT YOU WILL
PRAY AND GET CLOSER TO HIM.
JESUS WILL DO THINGS FOR US.

THE DEVIL FILL FIGHT US HARDER.
STOP HIM WITH GOD'S WORD.
THINGS TAKE TIME TO CHANGE.

GOD WILL CHANGE THINGS FOR US.
WE WILL ENJOY LIFE BETTER.
REMEMBER, GOD'S WORD.

**KEEP YOUR EYES ON JESUS.
ASK FOR JESUS' BLOOD TO
KEEP YOU SAFE FROM EVIL.**

WE NEED A CLEAN HEART EVERY DAY.
HE WILL COME BACK TO TAKE US.
WE WILL BE WITH HIM IN HEAVEN.

JESUS CALLS US TO BE KINGS
AND PRIESTS FOR HIM.
HE CHOSE US TO RULE WITH HIM.

JESUS WILL TAKE HIS BRIDE. THE BRIDE ARE PEOPLE WHO LIVE FULLY FOR JESUS.

SALVATION PRAYER

God, I know I sinned against you. Forgive me for the wrong that I have done. I believe that Jesus Christ died on the cross for me. That He rose from the grave so that after three days. I can have His long-lasting life. Come into my heart to be my Lord and Savior. I choose to turn away from my sins and I choose to follow you. Lead me to walk with you. Keep me safe and teach me your ways. Stop every bad thing in my life that has an open door to hurt me. Close those doors. Holy Spirit, fill me now in Jesus' name. Amen.

BAPTISM IN THE HOLY SPIRIT

Jesus, you are the one that fills me with Your Spirit. Come Holy Spirit and come into my life and fill me to overflow with Your presence. Come with your fire too. Thank you for the gift of tongues in Jesus' name. Amen.

Open your mouth and let the words come out that God gives you. It will be words that you don't know what they mean. You can ask God what it means. You need to let Him talk through you every day to grow this gift.

He will bring you closer to God and you will know Jesus more. You will have power from God to do great things and know things.

PRAYER

Thank you, Father God. I give my whole heart and my life. I want to love you more than the things in this world and more than anyone. Holy Spirit, help me love Jesus fully. Make me ready when Jesus comes back for His bride. Teach me how to walk by faith and obey Your word. Bring me to the people and places you want me to go. Make me pure and holy for you, in Jesus' name. Amen.

Thank you for reading this book. I hope you can leave a good review to encourage me to write more books to teach children and adults. The Lord blesses you with all that you do. May you experience all his blessings in your life and for your family too. Please share this book with others. The Lord will bless you more.

OTHER PRODUCTS

Knowing God

How to Hear God's Voice

New Life in Jesus

Loving Israel

God's Gifts/Spiritual Talents

Meeting God

Word Power

Fruit of the Spirit

The Tabernacle

Bride for Jesus

A Life of Prayer

Live Free

Who am I in Jesus

Walk in Love

God's Favor

Man of God

Woman of God

How to Use Money

God's Wisdom

Fasting

See Jerusalem and Bethany

First Fruit Offering

Feast of Trumpets

Day of Atonement

Feast of Tabernacles

Counting the Omer

Festival of Lights

Glory, Presence, and Holy Spirit

Live in God's Presence

Pentecost

See Galilee, Nazareth, and Tiberias

Hear God Speak

Knowing Jesus

Knowing Holy Spirit

A Healthy Life and Healthy Life Work Book

Smokey the Cat

Passover Unleavened Bread

Resurrection Life

The Blessing

Revival

Chelsea Learns Hebrew

Thanksgiving

Give Thanks

Jesus Birth

Loving Jesus: Bride and Groom

Proverbs 31 Woman

OTHER PRODUCTS

ABC of People in the Bible

Colours in the Bible

Breakthroughs

Open Doors

The Seven Spirits of God

Numbers in the Bible

Aglee the Eagle

An Eagle's Life

Chelsea Learns Numbers in Hebrew

ABC's of Faith

Feast of Purim

A Royal Life

Family Day

Family Blessings

Chinese New Year

Devotionals

31 Day Devotional

Inspirational/Other

Chelsea's Psalms and Poems

Your Daily Meal: Chelsea's Photo Album

Chelsea's Psalms and Poems2

Travel West Caribbean

Puzzle Books

Biblical Puzzle Book Vol 1-5

Bible Puzzles for Young Children Book 1-3

Biblical Puzzle for Children Books 1-5

Chelsea's Bible Puzzles

Teaching Series

How to Hear God's Voice Teaching Guide & Audio Book

Relationship with God, Jesus, Holy Spirit Guide

Knowing God, Jesus, Holy Spirit Guide & Audio Book

Flowing in the Prophetic

Teaching (Non-Sale on my website)

Purim

Passover

Resurrection

BOOK REVIEWS

More books on Amazon, Kobo, and Barnes and Noble, Smashwords, and IngramSpark.
https://chelseak532002550.wordpress.com/

More books on Amazon, Kobo, and Barnes and Noble, Smashwords, and IngramSpark.
https://www.amazon.com/author/chelseakong

Please leave a review and share with friends to help the author continue to write more books to reach more readers. Thank you so much for your support.

Review!

About
CHELSEA KONG

She is a writer, creative arts and digital media artist, skilled administration and certified PCP (Payroll Compliance Professional), and podcaster. Chelsea also served in a variety of roles, from audiovisual, photography, to assisting on the worship team, and ministry team. She also has a passion for families being united.

Chelsea has been a guest on Unity Live Radio, The Lady Tracey Show, and How to Live for Christ and is highly recommended by a Proud Christian blog. She is also a guest blogger. A few of her books have been featured in YourAuthorHub, etc. She graduated from Hotel and Restaurant Management, Digital Media Arts, Office Administration, Payroll Compliance Professional, and experience working with children. Chelsea lives in Toronto, Canada. She mainly writes children's books, stories, bridal writing, poems, lyrics for songs, words of encouragement, blessings, prayers, and jokes. The author of How to Hear the Voice of God, the Bridal Collection, Knowing God, etc. She also has her own Bible Puzzle books and other inspired products. Her podcast channel is called Chelsea K on Anchor, Spotify, and iTunes.

Please check my website to find out more:
https://chelseak532002550.wordpress.com/

www.ingramcontent.com/pod-product-compliance
Lightning Source LLC
LaVergne TN
LVHW072135070426
835513LV00003B/105